Five Year Life

82 Question Quiz To Make Sure Your
Life Planning And Your Career Planning
Are Congruent

#1 Amazon Bestseller In Job Hunting!

#1 Amazon Bestseller In
Personal Transformation!

Take Control - Discover How To Define
YOUR Future Life – How To Define Your
Future Point B

By

Robert Lee Goodman, MBA
www.FiveYearLife.com

Five Year Life TM Copyright Notice / Disclaimer

Version FYL – Print 2.0

By Robert Lee Goodman, MBA

Published by Good–Man LLC, Pox 3051,
Clearwater Beach, Florida 33767

ISBN: 978-0-9792952-3-2   0-9792952-3-8

For information, comments and suggestions, please contact Robert Lee Goodman at www.Chiefi.com or by direct e-mail to Robert@FiveYearLife.com.

Notice

This book is designed to provide information about telecommuting careers and home based businesses. Every effort has been made to make this book as complete and as accurate as possible, but no warranty is implied. Please exercise caution when considering any business or employment opportunity; you are assuming full responsibility for any outcome resulting from responding to the contents of this book.

No part of this publication may be reproduced or transmitted in any form or by any means, mechanical or electronic, including photocopying or recording, or by any information storage and retrieval system, or transmitted by email without permission in writing from the author.

While all attempts have been made to verify the information provided in this publication, neither the author nor the publisher assumes any responsibility for errors, omissions, or contrary interpretations of the subject matter herein.

This publication is not intended for use as any source of advice such as legal or accounting. The publisher wants to stress that the information contained herein may be subject to varying international, federal, state, and/or local laws or regulations. The purchaser or reader of this publication assumes responsibility for the use of these materials and information.

Adherence to all applicable laws and regulations, including international, federal, state and local governing professional licensing, business practices, advertising, and all other aspects of doing business in the US, Canada or any other jurisdiction is the sole responsibility of the purchaser or reader. Neither the author nor the publisher assume any responsibility or liability whatsoever on the behalf of the purchaser or reader of these materials.

All recordings and all associated documents are copyrighted by Ceo Resource LLC. All rights reserved. All materials contained in this audio recording and all associated documents are protected by copyright and trademark and shall not be used for any purpose whatsoever other

DISCLAIMER

CEO RESOURCE LLC DOES NOT OFFER LEGAL OR TAX ADVICE OF ANY KIND WHATSOEVER – JUST GENERAL BUSINESS ADVICE. AS A CONSEQUENCE, CEO RESOURCE OFFERS ABSOLUTELY NO ASSURANCE WHATSOEVER THAT THESE, OR ANY OF ITS DOCUMENTS, IN CURRENT FORM, ITS AUDIOS OR ANY OTHER ADVICE ARE COMPLIANT, IN ANY WAY, WITH ANY OR ALL STATE OR FEDERAL LAWS. ALL DOCUMENTS FROM CEO RESOURCE SHOULD ONLY BE CONSIDERED SAMPLES ONLY FOR BUSINESS EDUCATION AND SHOULD NOT BE USED IN ANY WAY PRIOR TO A COMPREHENSIVE REVIEW BY YOUR OWN ATTORNEY.

The sample documents are provided for information purposes only and are not intended to replace legal advice offered by legal counsel. Readers are strongly encouraged to consult competent legal counsel before using any of the sample documents. Your use of the sample documents is at your sole risk. Ceo Resource LLC assumes no responsibility relating to the use of the sample documents and Ceo Resource LLC, its officers, directors, employees and attorneys hereby disclaim any responsibility whatsoever for, or any liability resulting from, the use of the sample documents.

For Janet

For all of our wonderful five-year chapters

Past, present and future...

TABLE OF CONTENTS

*"The future depends on
what we do in the present."*

– Mahatma Gandhi.

FIVE YEAR LIFE - YOUR PERSONAL PLAN

I have two apparently disparate careers: one, as an internationally-known management consultant to startup and emerging companies – two, as a relationship expert and published author of a book called, "Efficient Love."

Even though this combination may seem strange, these two parallel careers are really not as dissimilar as they might first appear.

These two different personal focal points share a common, passionate mission of mine: Helping people get from their current Point A to their desired Point B - for both their personal life and their business life.

After three decades of experience pursuing this mission, I've learned a few axioms of life that I want to share with you:

- Too many folks never consider that they have control of their own destiny. As a result, they never know where they're going – and they end up taking too many dead-end trails that lead to nowhere because they never understood they had the right and the ability to choose their Point B.

🕰 **T**oo many folks procrastinate even the micro-decisions that affect their life path. As a result, they are frozen by indecisiveness when it comes to the big decisions because they never take responsibility for defining their own Point B.

🕰 **T**oo many folks consider two weeks to be long term planning. As a result, they end up making reflex decisions that get them off the right path because they never defined their right Point B past a two-week timeline.

🕰 **I**f you are already in a long-term relationship, you and your significant-other need to have a similar desired Point B destination and a shared path to reach it.

🕰 **I**f you don't, at some point your paths will probably go different directions to the point that each of you may end up going your separate ways. This is discussed in great detail in my #1 Amazon Bestseller book, "Efficient Love" - so, if you need more information about this, buy the book at Amazon.com.

You and your career goals need to have a similar desired Point B destination. If you are even considering starting a company, your very first decision needs to be your definition of the right-for-your personal Point B. Not everyone is cut out to be an entrepreneur — and it may make a lot more sense, for a lot

of reasons, for you to work for someone else. Even then, your career decisions need to be congruent with your personal Point B.

The choice between starting and running a company - versus working for someone else's company will depend upon what is right for you. But either way, your personal desired Point B needs to be on the same path as your business Point B -- or you will have dragons galore that will need to be slayed on a regular basis.

Part of my personal mission is to help you make sure you're on the right path to YOUR desired Point B - helping you define what is right for you.

"PAYING IT FORWARD"
TO THE WORLD

The premise of my personal mission is: If folks will freely choose and fully define their DESIRED Point B, they are much more likely to reach their DESIRED Point B.

I use the following Quiz as a starting point for most all of my consulting clients -- whether it's for Efficient Love or my management consulting related to starting or growing a company. Until I know my clients' real and personal Point B, I can't fully understand how to give them the very best help possible.

But beyond this business use, I strongly believe that everyone can greatly benefit from this methodology. Every man, woman and near-adult child can use this basic approach to more fully take control of their own lives.

I've been using this Quiz with business clients and relationship clients alike for the past 15 years. During that time, it has been gratifying to see the overwhelming, positive impact it has had on so many folks.

Because of these successes, I already know this process can help those who approach it with an open mind.

Because these issues are so important to virtually everyone's life, I want to make this Workbook available to everyone - so you can realistically take control of your life and find the congruent path to your own personal Point B.

It is my way of "paying it forward" to the world -- whether we ever do business together or not.

If this Quiz even helps you have one insight that will help you get more quickly to YOUR desired Point B, then that is the key reward I want.

ARE YOU AT ONE OF LIFE'S CROSSROADS?

Five Year Life was specifically written to positively and pivotally affect lives – especially those who are currently at one of life's many crossroads.

Are you, or someone you know, facing major life changes and choices such as:

- **S**tudents and graduates?

- **T**hose who are dating, marrying or divorcing?

- **T**hose who are job hunting, have lost their job, changing careers or starting their own business?

- **T**hose who are seeking personal transformation?

- **T**hose who are re-evaluating their lives for a variety of other reasons?

If so, then Five Year Life will be especially and immediately meaningful to your present and future.

One of my favorite quotes by Mahatma Gandhi was at the beginning of this book, "The future depends on what we do in the present."

What are you going to do in your present, starting now, to positively affect your future and your path to your most personally desired Point B?

SAVING MANKIND ONE MILLION YEARS

My goal is to get this life-changing book into the hands of at least a million readers who are committed to taking control of their lives in order to reach their own personal point B destination.

If I can save each of those committed reader from wasting just one year, then one million books might save mankind a MILLION YEARS from folks squandering time and life on wrong paths caused by incompatibilities with their personal, career and relationship goals.

If I can reach that goal, I believe the result will be a lot of increased happiness and fulfillment in the world.

As you read through these questions, consider what new ideas, thoughts and epiphanies that you gain about your Point B that could end up saving you at least one year of YOUR life - a year that you might've otherwise wasted on a dead-end trail.

If I can save you a year, or more, of your life, then I believe we both have successfully benefited from your investment in Five Year Life.

I would genuinely love to hear from you about your successes and epiphanies that you gain from reading and implementing Five Year Life.

Please e-mail your comments and stories directly to me at Robert@FiveYearLife.com. Thanks!

CONGRUENCY

I promise this won't take long – but the next 30 minutes might possibly give you some life changing epiphanies. Such as: Does your new company or career REALLY fit the lifestyle you say is important to you and your family?

Consider your personal gain if even one of these epiphanies, or even one "Ah Ha" moment of clarity, gives you the right answer to a pivotal question BEFORE you start your new company, change jobs or hook up in that next romantic relationship?

Wouldn't even one epiphany be a great ROI for this 30 minute investment of your time?

In the following 30 minute Quiz, stop all of your multiplexing for a few minutes. Instead, think about you.

- **W**hat are YOU going to be doing five years from today?

- **W**hat will be your ideal Five Year Life?

- **W**hat are the right tactical and strategic decisions for YOU?

Unless you know where you WANT to go in your personal life, it's going to be difficult to make a lot of the right business and personal decisions that you will face every day, week and year between now and five years from now.

If you're getting ready to start a new company, you're getting ready to start down a long path that might lead to success and riches – or failure and ruin. Your journey down this path may consume a good portion of the next year or even decades of your life.

Whether you're starting a new company or are working for someone else's company, the question is still the same:

Are you going to end up with a business life that is totally congruent with your personal needs – and the needs of your family?

SOME SIMPLE QUESTIONS

I'd like to share with you a valuable thought process that might give you some critical insights into your personal future. The questions are very simple.

It's the answers that will affect the rest of your life.

And, yes, I know this may sound like the same trite question you probably got on your first job interview.

But that was when you were a kid. With all that you have now experienced, you should have the insight to answer the questions with your current goals in mind.

JUST ANOTHER DAY –
IN THE LIFE OF YOU

Try to realistically project, in writing with as much detail as possible, the details for a typical day in your life five years from today.

In other words, what will be your Five Year Life?

Picture a typical day – the way you really want it. The more details you can include, the better the image will be of what you really want to work toward.

Bear in mind that I'm just talking about a typical day – like the second Tuesday of each month.

Nothing special.

Nothing out of the ordinary.

Just life the way you want it to really be – on that second Tuesday of each month.

However, I'm not talking about some probably unobtainable fantasy where you are a rock star or an astronaut – or have replaced Warren Buffett as one of the richest men on Earth.

But, I'm also not talking about a simple extension of what your life is now.

Instead, do a zero–based projection – starting from scratch – that would be realistic for you – with your real preferences as the important parts of a typical day in your life.

Just as a guide, let me suggest a few questions that might stimulate others that are even more applicable for you.

Note: This is your life and career planning Workbook.

You have complete permission to write and scribble your ideas, notes, action plan, etc. anywhere and everywhere throughout this book. That's what it's designed for.

I've even included a couple of dozen blank pages at the end of the book so that you have plenty of room to capture all of your visions for your Point B. That way you can look back from the future at your today answers.

EIGHTY TWO QUESTIONS – OR MORE - ABOUT YOUR DESIRED FIVE YEAR LIFE

What time will you wake up?

....

....

....

....

....

Who do you wake up next to?

....

....

....

....

....

What is your morning ritual?

....

....

....

....

....

How many kids are still waking up in the same house?

....

....

....

....

....

What kind of house is it?

....

....

....

....

....

Where is the house located?

....

....

....

....

....

In the city or in the suburbs?

....

....

....

....

....

What city is closest?

....

....

....

....

How big is your house?

....

....

....

....

What does it look like?

....

....

....

....

What kind of view do you see out the windows?

....

....

....

....

....

What will be your monthly household budget?

....

....

....

....

....

What will be your social lifestyle?

....

....

....

....

....

What time do you leave for the office?

....

....

....

....

....

Or, will you be retired?

....

....

....

....

....

How enthusiastic will you be to leave home and go to the office?

....

....

....

....

....

What kind of car will you drive to work?

How far do you drive?

How long does it take?

⏳ **O**r, will you be taking some kind of public transit?

....

....

....

....

....

⏳ **O**r, will you just go into your office at the house and telecommute?

....

....

....

....

....

⏳ **H**ow much traveling will you be doing for business?

....

....

....

....

....

To where?

....

....

....

....

....

How many days a month will you be gone?

....

....

....

....

....

What kind of office do you have?

....

....

....

....

....

What does it look like?

....

....

....

....

....

What part of town is it in?

....

....

....

....

What town?

....

....

....

....

What do you see out the windows?

....

....

....

....

....

What business are you in, then?

....

....

....

....

....

Will it be the same as it is today?

....

....

....

....

....

Will your business have evolved into something completely different?

....

....

....

....

....

What part of the business will take most of your time?

....

....

....

....

....

How many people will you have working for you?

....

....

....

....

....

How many of them do you see during the day?

....

....

....

....

....

How many will be reporting directly to you?

....

....

....

....

....

How many meetings will you attend?

....

....

....

....

....

How much time will you spend on the phone?

....

....

....

....

....

How many customers will you have?

....

....

....

....

....

What will be your annual revenues?

....

....

....

....

....

How will you spend lunch time?

....

....

....

....

....

What will be the parts of the job that will give you the most pleasure?

....

....

....

....

....

What parts will be your biggest hassles?

....

....

....

....

....

Will your ideal business in five years, be your ideal business five years after that?

....

....

....

....

....

What dragons will you be slaying on a regular basis?

....

....

....

....

....

What will you be doing that will be wasting too much of your time?

....

....

....

....

....

What parts of your job will make you feel strong?

....

....

....

....

....

What parts of your job will make you feel weak?

....

....

....

....

....

What parts of your day will you dread most?

....

....

....

....

....

How many hours a day, a week, will you typically be working?

....

....

....

....

....

What will be your personal financial situation in five years?

....

....

....

....

....

Your take home pay?

....

....

....

....

....

⧗ **Y**our personal net worth?

....

....

....

....

....

⧗ **W**hat level of debt will you have?

....

....

....

....

⧗ **W**hat major expenses will you face?

....

....

....

....

Will you be supporting children in college or be supporting your parents or both?

....

....

....

....

....

How much will you have saved for retirement?

....

....

....

....

....

What financial protection will you have in case of catastrophe?

....

....

....

....

....

What investments will you have made?

....

....

....

....

....

What time will you leave the office?

....

....

....

....

Where do you go when you leave?

....

....

....

....

How anxious are you to go home?

....

....

....

....

....

What time do you get home?

....

....

....

....

....

Who will be there when you get home?

....

....

....

....

....

What will you do for dinner?

....

....

....

....

....

How will you spend the week night evenings?

....

....

....

....

....

What time will you go to bed?

....

....

....

....

....

What civic or children or other activities will you be involved with?

....

....

....

....

....

What hobbies or past times will occupy some of your time?

....

....

....

....

....

What will you really do on a regular basis to give back to society, community and mankind?

....

....

....

....

....

What will you really do on a regular basis to be a better spouse, parent, child and friend?

....

....

....

....

....

What else about your desired life should you list here?

....

....

....

....

....

ALL OF THOSE ARE JUST THE DAY IN, DAY OUT, ROUTINES OF LIFE.

Now Add These:

How do you spend your next 260 weekends?

....

....

....

....

....

What will you do on your next half–dozen vacations?

....

....

....

....

....

How often will you take off from work for long weekends?

....

....

....

....

....

How often will you take a real vacation?

....

....

....

....

....

What special events happen in those 260 weeks that equal your life for the next five years?

....

....

....

....

....

What will be the routine of your life?

....

....

....

....

....

What will be your punctuation marks?

....

....

....

....

....

What other things will be important to you, to your lifestyle, five years from now?

....

....

....

....

....

What are the top 100 changes you should make now - to have life the way you want it then?

....

....

....

....

....

What excuses do you think you have from starting those changes today?

....

....

....

....

Can you get where you want to be faster than five years?

....

....

....

....

....

What else about your desired life should you list here?

....

....

....

....

....

RINSE AND REPEAT

· ·

Now, go back and reread this same list – except this time, start penciling out the easy answers to the questions in the Workbook.

Next, go back one last time and reread the same list – except this time, penciling in other questions that relate to your life, your lifestyle, your family, your vision for your personal future.

ALL IN THE FAMILY

Now, if you already have a spouse, girlfriend, boyfriend or significant-other with whom you plan to share your future Five Year Life, I strongly recommend you have them take this same Quiz – BEFORE you show them your answers.

It might be even interesting to see how your own kids, if you have them, would answer the same questions – again, without them seeing your answers first.

Since these are the people who will probably be in your life five years from today, it may be worthwhile getting their opinion. They may want to vote on whether or not you should take the path you're getting ready to choose for you.

You might not want to give them the vote on this matter – but be prepared for the consequences of path incompatibility with the people who are currently important in your life.

DIFFERENT ANSWERS

There are, of course, no wrong answers to any of these questions.

Just different answers...

But, short of catastrophe, five years from today WILL happen. You might as well choose the direction and the destination you want.

The journey has already started.

"THE ONLY THING WORSE..."

One of my favorite proverbs is, "The only thing worse than going the wrong direction, is going the wrong direction enthusiastically!"

Many of us love doing things enthusiastically. However, if we go charging off in the wrong direction, at some point in we have to stop, turn around and retrace our steps back to Point A - and start all over again.

The upshot of starting over again is that all the time, energy, effort and money you just spent going down that dead-end trail is mostly wasted – the time spent going the wrong direction delays your successful implementation of your vision and getting to your desired Point B.

It also means that you need more money, more time, more effort than you would have otherwise needed if you had done a better job of planning and picking the right direction to begin with.

That's really the purpose of this Quiz.

Even if you just do a little bit of work answering each of these 82 or more questions...even if you only generate a couple of dozen action items... even if you only make sweeping assumptions about your life between now and five years from now, you're probably going to be much better off because you've eliminated at least some of those wrong directions.

The more time you spend on these 82 questions, the more wrong directions will get eliminated. The more wrong directions that get eliminated, the much more likely will be your success at achieving your desired Point B.

So, what's it worth to you?

How many hours are you willing to invest in thinking about the answers to these questions in order to eliminate as many wrong directions as you possibly can? One? Five? Ten? Hundred?

How many hours, months or years are you going to waste, otherwise, cleaning up the mess from not doing it right the first time?

It's your life. Make a major investment in you.

THE NEXT STEP IS NOW

Figure out where you are right now.

Then, decide what you have to do, what you have to change, to end up at the destination you really want.

The best way to do this is develop an action plan for each and every answer you have for these 82 questions.

No arm waving allowed. This is what separates out this approach from the "feel good" crowd of coaches – have a specific action plan to get you to EACH of your Point B answers.

Like my other Pop Quizzes, these questions can seem deceptively simple until you consider all the implications of your answers.

Hopefully, this Quiz will be a catalyst to help you generate even more pertinent questions that specifically relate to you and your current and desired reality.

ROBERT'S RULE OF ORDER:

If You Want To End Up Someplace West
Does It Make Sense To Keep Heading East?

NEED HELP?

As you go through each of those 82 or more questions and consider the impact of each answer on your Five Year Life, you may find you need help with the decision making or the implementation steps required to really get you to your desired Point B.

Each month, I try to set aside at least a few hours to offer one-on-one mentoring and coaching to those who are genuinely focused on reaching their desired Point B.

If you are interested in this kind of help, either for your career or your relationships, please check out my web site at www.ConsultantOptions. com for information on my coaching and mentoring services. There, you will find information on my rates and availability.

Again, my mission is to help clients reach their own desired Point B as quickly as possible.

If you can get there by yourself using these 82 questions as a catalyst, that is fantastic! Seek out epiphanies for yourself in every question. Lay out an action plan for each answer you give.

You might, just maybe, find that many of your answers can be achieved very quickly. You may find that many of the answers that define your desired Point B can be achieved in a week, a month or a year – not Five Years.

Start now - you might surprise yourself with just how fast you'll start enjoying the Five Year Life you want most.

Warm regards,

Robert Lee Goodman, MBA
Ceo & Chief ImpleMentor
www.Chiefi.com
www.FiveYearLife.com

PS: If you find this Workbook helpful, please leave a review on the book's Amazon page.

NOTES, IDEAS AND ACTION PLANNING FOR YOUR FIVE YEAR LIFE

• •

Use the following few dozen blank pages to fill in the blanks in your own Five Year Life.

These are not filler pages to make this book seem bigger. These blank pages are meant to give you plenty of room to turn this book into a living, breathing Workbook about you and your future Five Year Life.

Add your hand-written notes as you drill down on your own right answers to each of the questions in this book – along with your answers to all the other questions that I hope that this book generates that are uniquely yours about your vision of your future.

The more details you add to your written notes, the better your visualization. The better your visualization of your future, the higher your probability will be of reaching your own personal Point B.

You might consider carrying this book with you so that when you have a few minutes of down time or wait time you can scribble your answers to questions and other thoughts - even if it is just for one question, just for one thought, just for one idea or action item.

If you do this, you may be pleasantly surprised how fast your blanks for you Five Year Life get answered and fine-tuned.

Control your own destiny – Starting now.

NOTES, IDEAS & ACTION ITEMS

Always Think Outside This Box Too!

NOTES, IDEAS & ACTION ITEMS

Always Think Outside This Box Too!

NOTES, IDEAS & ACTION ITEMS

Always Think Outside This Box Too!

NOTES, IDEAS & ACTION ITEMS

Always Think Outside This Box Too!

NOTES, IDEAS & ACTION ITEMS

Always Think Outside This Box Too!

NOTES, IDEAS & ACTION ITEMS

Always Think Outside This Box Too!

NOTES, IDEAS & ACTION ITEMS

Always Think Outside This Box Too!

NOTES, IDEAS & ACTION ITEMS

Always Think Outside This Box Too!

NOTES, IDEAS & ACTION ITEMS

Always Think Outside This Box Too!

NOTES, IDEAS & ACTION ITEMS

Always Think Outside This Box Too!

NOTES, IDEAS & ACTION ITEMS

Always Think Outside This Box Too!

NOTES, IDEAS & ACTION ITEMS

Always Think Outside This Box Too!

NOTES, IDEAS & ACTION ITEMS

Always Think Outside This Box Too!

NOTES, IDEAS & ACTION ITEMS

Always Think Outside This Box Too!

NOTES, IDEAS & ACTION ITEMS

Always Think Outside This Box Too!

NOTES, IDEAS & ACTION ITEMS

Always Think Outside This Box Too!

NOTES, IDEAS & ACTION ITEMS

Always Think Outside This Box Too!

NOTES, IDEAS & ACTION ITEMS

Always Think Outside This Box Too!

ABOUT THE AUTHOR

Robert Lee Goodman, MBA is CEO and Chief ImpleMentor at Ceo Resource LLC, a worldwide consulting company focused solely on startup and emerging companies.

During the past 20 years, Ceo Resource LLC, has already helped, on a one-on-one basis, THOUSANDS of diverse start up and emerging companies and their CEOs in 49 of the 50 states in more than 46 countries on six of the seven continents with their business and sales and marketing planning, strategy and tactics, action planning, problem solving, fundraising and plan implementation.

Robert's elevator pitch: "I Help Startup Companies Plan, Strategize, Fund And Implement Their Vision By Becoming A Virtual, Part-Time, Interim Executive Of Their Company."

After completing his MBA, Robert successfully started four dozen of his own companies, hiring hundreds of employees and raising $25 million from over 1,200 investors and venture capital firms. Some of these companies included:

- **A** $100 million real estate investment company with a diverse portfolio – buying everything from apartment complexes to office buildings, office warehouses and mini warehouses.

- **A**n asset management company subsidiary with operations in five states overseeing 45,000 rental units.

- **H**e built one of his companies into the seventh largest self-storage operation in the nation.

- **A** software company with products on the shelves of 5,000 retail outlets nationwide. He wrote the first program, for real estate investment analysis, staffed the company with about 50 great folks, and ended up taking the company public with a reverse merger into a public shell.

- **A** financial services company buying defaulted loans from the FDIC and RTC for five cents on the dollar after the debacle caused by the Tax Reform Act back in 1986.

- **A**n NASD broker-dealer company, raising $25 million from angel investors and VC for his own companies.

Mr. Goodman's Virtual Chief Operating Officer and Virtual Executive Services include: starting, managing and operating all or part of a company, venture capital and private placement fund raising, handling securities issues and investor relations, business development, financial analysis, mergers and acquisitions, tactical and strategic sale, marketing and business planning, real estate consulting and mentoring -- along with providing additional, seasoned senior management experience - especially in a pre-IPO environment.

His background also includes a Master of Business Administration, Presidential & Key Executive Program, from Pepperdine University and a Bachelor of Science, cum laude, in Engineering Physics, from the University of Tennessee.

Robert's web site is www.ChiefImpleMentor.com and he can be reached with the contact form at that site.

Robert and his wife Janet live on the shores of the Gulf of Mexico on Sand Key Island, Clearwater Beach Florida.

This is part of their Five Year Life.

BOOKS BY ROBERT LEE GOODMAN

Robert is a bestselling author with several works available at Amazon. com:

Five Year Life - #1 Amazon Bestseller! Take Control – Discover How To Define YOUR Future Life – Define Your Future Point B. What are you doing in YOUR present Point A to get to YOUR five year future Point B?

Efficient Love - #1 Amazon Bestseller! A Step-By-Step Guide For Efficiently Finding Your Own Happily Ever After! Efficient Love is intended to help you take charge of your own Quest. Get the power to create your own "Happily Here & Now" and "Happily Ever After" in the ways that are most meaningful for you. Efficiently!

Don't Waste Another Sunset - Amazon Bestseller For Short Stories! Five short stories with each one centered around a very different woman who pursued her own personal quest for her version of happily ever after.

101 Questions For Your Startup Company - #1 Amazon Bestseller! Before you are ready to produce a meaningful business plan for your startup or emerging company, you need to have thought through a series of pivotal issues in order to end up with a realistic plan for implementation.

Funding Foreplay - #1 Amazon Bestseller! Funding Foreplay is a training course that teaches startup company CEOs like you - how to properly prepare and present the dozen documents you must have to successfully romance and seduce angel investors and VC to invest in your company.

NOTES, IDEAS & ACTION ITEMS
Always Think Outside This Box Too!